Lecturing to
LARGE GROUPS

by L. S. Powell

Deputy Principal,
Garnett College of Education (Technical)

Published by
British Association for Commercial and Industrial Education
16 Park Crescent, London W1N 4AP   Tel: 01-636 5351

Lecturing to
LARGE GROUPS

In short, over-indulgence in being lectured to is a primrose path to intellectual sloth, the more fatally deceitful because it looks virtuous.
  Sir Arthur Quiller-Couch: A Lecture on Lectures: *Hogarth Press: London,* 1927.

Lectures were once useful; but now, when all can read, and books are so numerous, lectures are unnecessary.
  Dr. Johnson: from Boswell, Life of Johnson.

THE LECTURE IS THE MOST FREQUENTLY AND strongly criticised form of communication for learning.* Every tutor who discusses lectures with his students knows that much of their content is forgotten after a short interval of time. And yet the lecture persists. Is it indeed too inefficient to be of value?

A series of experiments comparing the lecture and lesson techniques for introducing the binary system to adults carried out by the author gave results in favour of the lecture (despite the original intention of showing the superiority of the lesson!). Following up the correspondence initiated by certain public lectures testifies to the very active response that they are capable of evoking. Perhaps it is not the technique which is at fault but the purposes for which it is employed.

Those who condemn the lecture advocate more active participation by group members. Josephine Klein in her book *Working with Groups*[1] opens her second chapter with the following anecdote:

Two psychologists wrote to all those who had been present at a meeting of the British Psychological Society and asked them what they could remember of the recent discussion ... only a tenth of the points that had been made were recalled in the reports. Of these, nearly half were 'substantially incorrect', ... The average member was, however, no more accurate about (points he had contributed) himself than he was about others.

The opponents of lecturing hold that few people

---

*See for example Chapter 3 of *Educating Older People* by M. F. Cleugh. *Tavistock Publications.*
1. *Working with Groups* by Josephine Klein. Hutchinson, London, 1961.

are capable of really good lecturing, that the lecture often invites insincerity and showing off on the part of the lecturer and posing on the part of the audience and, perhaps more important, that it does not fulfil a truly educative function since it represses the learner's initiative and reduces his role to that of a recipient of ideas instead of an active participant in their generation.

Many of the pronouncements made on the relative effectiveness of different modes of communication take no account of the widths of the spectra of abilities, subjects and circumstances. No critic would regard the physically passive audience at a symphony concert as ill-served nor would he assess the success of the performance by testing for the retention of certain phrases taken out of context. Some groups of ideas are akin to the coherent sequence in a symphony and can be presented only by sustained and delicately balanced arguments which are more readily comprehensible to some people when they are heard than when they are read. In such circumstances the lecture is an appropriate mode of presentation. Here the lecturer demonstrates how he, the master craftsman as it were, produces his masterpieces. He can show the sequence, draw attention to the pitfalls, highlight that which is of great significance because he knows so well. To chop up such a demonstration (by discussion technique, for example), however well the joints may be concealed, presents the audience with something different from the whole in the same way as a symphony played in instalments would be different in quality from the whole. In this case the learners are responding to and developing the discipline which lies behind the capacity to be creative.

The Report of the University Grants Committee[2] on methods summarized the evidence in favour of lectures as follows:

Immature university students learn more readily by listening than by reading;
Lectures are especially valuable for introducing and opening up a subject and students can thus be led into

subjects which would otherwise prove too daunting for them;

It is easier to coordinate lectures (than tutorials etc) and laboratory work;

Where knowledge is advancing rapidly textbooks may not be available;

Lectures awaken a critical attitude in students;

Lectures can provide aesthetic pleasure;

Inspiring teachers, by lecturing, can infect far more students;

Lectures are economical of staff time.

This report referred to university lectures in 1964 when 10 per cent of groups attending lectures numbered less than five students and 6 per cent of groups were over 100. In the next year the Robbins Committee[3] stated it saw little value in formal lectures delivered to small audiences.

The American Committee on the Utilisation of College Teaching Resources[4] did not support the widely-held view that small classes were essential to the most efficient learning. It stated that 'more students are capable of working independently of classroom instruction than have been given the opportunity . . . but they require to be prepared for independent study to get the fullest benefit from it'. As part of this preparation for independent study, the Committee included lecturing to very large groups by good lecturers. It strongly recommended that every institution should be organized to provide for groups of a wide variety of sizes including very large ones. (See also references 5 and 6).

As with kissing, clinical tests can prove that lecturing is a 'bad thing'. Indeed, the comparison can be taken further. Those who have never participated in a good lecture cannot know its power to inspire: its full impact can only be appreciated by consenting adults; its effectiveness is usually dependent in part upon effective visual aids. And, furthermore, despite all the protests, it is going to remain an important mode of communication for a considerable time to come.

---

2. *University Teaching Methods: Report of the University Grants Committee.* HMSO, London, 1965. (The '*Hale Report*').
3. *The Report of the Committee on Higher Education.* HMSO, London, 1965. (The '*Robbins Report*').
4. *Better Utilisation of College Teaching Resources.* The Fund for the Advancement of Education, New York, USA, 1959.
5. *The Crisis in the University* by W. Moberley. SCM Press, London, 1949.
6. *Redbrick University* by B. Truscott. *Faber*, London, 1943.

The special quality of a successful lecture to a large group is the air of occasion which surrounds it – the size of the lecture hall, the shifting groupings of people, the shuffling hush of conversation which snuffs out as the proceedings begin, the vote of thanks and the applause. This is more than somebody talking to people. The lecture content too is special. It will have been prepared, rehearsed, arranged and, if necessary, spiced with verbal asides or illustrations. A lecture is often the culmination of the work of many people: those who prepare the hall, invite the audience, control the lighting, check the acoustics, introduce the lecturer and cope with the wide range of details which escape notice unless they are overlooked.

The successful lecturer will have learned certain abilities. He will be able to exploit the responses special to crowds – those strange responses of expectancy, humour, inspiration and the like which can be evoked only with large audiences and which have their roots in some incomprehensible form of communication so highly developed in certain kinds of gregarious animals. His response to his audience and his accommodation to his subject are the strategies of the craft, not the rules. The strategies are the lecturer's personal interpretations and although they may be modified by his knowing the rules by which he should lecture they are not determined by them.

The rules of lecturing, on the other hand, the guidelines, are the procedures which are *generally* followed by successful lecturers. These include ways of structuring a lecture, how to stand and so on. But like the rules for happy marriages they may be broken by the most experienced of practitioners but should never be ignored by the novice.

The Purpose of a Lecture

In a successful lecture a person and a particular area of his competence are presented to a willing audience which is capable of assessing them critically. Matching the lecturer and his subject on the one hand with the audience on the other is essential to success since during a lecture there is no overt feed-back from the listeners, and although able lecturers sense *rapport*, and make adjustments to maximise it as they lecture, they should not be forced to make major modifications to their prepared plan. This throws the initial responsibility for success on the organiser who, in addition to his function as a promoter and manager, must also bring together a lecturer and audience which are compatible one with the other.

Fig. 1. *To reinforce motivation and give direction*

The purposes for which lectures are particularly suitable are:
1. To give a general idea of the scope and content of a subject which is to be studied in detail later;
2. To stimulate interest in a subject or line of action or thought;
3. To present a new thesis or technique;
4. To persuade people of their own capacity to understand or enjoy; and
5. To provide an aesthetically stimulating experience.

Lecture Settings

No lecture is every completely isolated as an experience although some may be unsupported by any formal preparation or recapitulation by the listeners. Such lectures, provided attendance at them is voluntary, and provided they are accurately advertised, can be stimulating sources of learning since, in general, they will be attended by audiences with an interest in the subject, or the speaker. Such lecture meetings should usually terminate with a discussion but, in general, this will serve only to clarify certain issues which were not quite

Fig. 2. *To Inspire and Teach*

clear to some people. This type of lecture, whilst it ostensibly provides information, should aim primarily at attitude-reinforcement. It caters for people who are interested enough to attend and are therefore likely to be willing to go further provided the lecture stimulates them to do so (*Fig.* 1). The contents of such lectures should be summarised in a handout or extended in a booklet. In many cases a bibliography will be valuable.

A lecture which is to be followed by seminars or group discussions* on the other hand can result in closely controlled learning (*Fig.* 2). Prior to the lecture, selected group-leaders will be briefed by the lecturer so that the essential content of his presentation will be consolidated. The two periods should be regarded as complementary and prepared for as one by the lecturer who should ensure that his audience anticipates the form of the follow-up period. The aim here is to direct

Fig. 3. *To Satisfy Desire to Know*

intellectual activity towards a predetermined goal through participation.

A third arrangement relegates the lecture itself to a secondary role: it forms the recapitulation of a more comprehensive paper prepared by the lecturer and circulated to the audience at least a week or so before the meeting (*Fig.* 3). The lecture in this case, either restates the main features of the paper in the form of a summary or supports them with different, but closely related, data. In this lecture form the personality of the lecturer should not intrude into the subject matter.

The duration of this form of lecture will tend to be short – about twenty minutes is often sufficient – in order to provide for a longer discussion than

---

*In an experiment to find the most suitable size of tutorial group for teaching efficiency carried out under Professor T. L. Cottrell of the University of Edinburgh in 1960-61 and 1961-62, groups of 12 students obtained more favourable scores than groups of either 3 or 24.

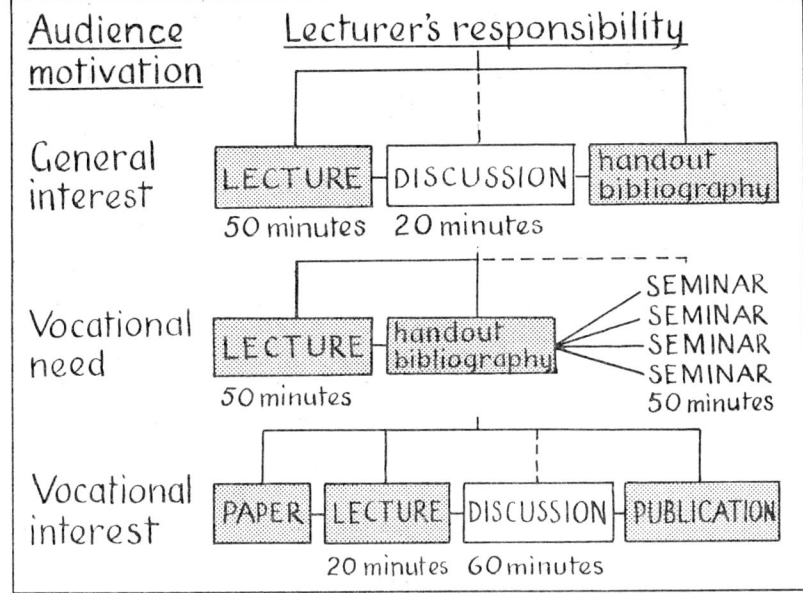

Fig. 4. *The three basic lecture settings;*
  General interest;
  Vocational need;
  Vocational interest

would otherwise be possible. The discussion is taken down and transcribed into typescript after which it is first circulated to the participants from the audience. When they have edited their contributions the paper is passed to the lecturer who corrects and edits his replies. The paper and discussion are then published. This form of lecture is suited to meetings of learned societies: it aims of publicising, extending, qualifying and assessing the lecturer's thesis.

The three basic lecture settings are summarised in *Fig.* 4.

Organisation

The decision to provide a lecture for a large group should not be taken lightly: if such a lecture fails, it fails many people with a great deal of publicity. It should begin perhaps three months before the actual day with an expression of need from potential members of the audience or from a decision by a committee or board. In reaching their decision, they should be precise about the nature of the audience, the object of the lecture and its financial implications if these are relevant. Against this data and using reliable information, the lecturer and chairman should be proposed.

From this point an organiser should take over and book the hall. He should then arrange for a responsible person to invite the lecturer and make a preliminary contact with the chairman. Many lecturers receive more requests to lecture than they can accept and they should therefore be approached in good time – a year in advance is not uncommon – and provided with concise but comprehensive information.

If the lecturer is a consultant he should be asked to state his fee and if he is a member of the teaching profession he should be offered a fee of about one two-hundredth of his annual income. (This equates one lecture to about a day's work). Within a school or college, a lecture of this kind should be regarded as the equivalent of at least three classroom periods. (Inspectors, directors and some company representatives are usually required to decline fees.)

The lecturer will usually need to know about his audience – their background, age-range and reasons for attending – the timing of the proceedings, the location of the hall and the route he should take to get there, the meal and hotel arrangements and, if possible, the name of his chairman. It helps some lecturers to be given a sketch plan of the hall, the position of the electrical sockets and their type, the kind of projection and display equipment available, the nearest car park and the name of the technical assistant or caretaker responsible for the hall. The ability to find good lecturers relates fairly closely to good management.

Designing a Lecture

Every lecture to a large group must be prepared with the greatest care. This work should fall into three phases – designing the form of the lecture, composing its content and organising its presentation: the lecturer is composer, conductor and orchestra rolled into one. Unfortunately some lecturers are satisfied if they do no more than mouth essays, turning what might have been interesting articles into, at best, unattractive and prolonged monologues.* Eminence should be no excuse for vocal vandalism.

Designing the form of a lecture involves the imagination. From time to time over days or weeks the lecture is visualised as one would visualise a play or a symphony. During this phase the lecturer will decide upon his 'line' and review his strategies. He should think about presenting his subject in such a way as to reveal what he feels and believes about it: in such a way as to make it *his* lecture. In this way he will give the occasion a dimension which is lacking in a printed article: it should be impossible to make a good lecture lie flat on a sheet of paper. This involvement of the lecturer is sometimes confused with the aim of the lecture but the concept of aim is too narrow and too objective to describe this decision. Thus we hear tell of 'A lecture by Bragg on . . .' rather than 'A lecture on . . .'.

From these thoughts the crude structure of the presentation will take shape; variations, recapitulations and illustrations will be considered in various settings until the general form becomes reasonably settled. Throughout this time the lecturer will keep his audience in mind: he will see them both as a group and as individuals: he will put himself in the place of a listener and ask how he would react. Page 7 shows some of the notes made during this period prior to a lecture on visual aids and page 8 shows them gathered together in readiness for the preparation of the lecture itself.

Preparation

Although practised professionals develop individual methods, beginners should write out their lectures fairly fully. A fifty minute lecture consists of about 5,000 words which, allowing for inevitable pauses, is a pace of about 110 words per minute. This means preparing about five pages of singly-spaced typescript on quarto paper.

Whilst the form of the lecture was being developed, content notes should have been made at the same time, never left to the last moment. These will include references to books and articles, to experiences, experiments and so on. When the lecture content is written, many of these ideas will be rejected since the essence of most good lectures is a structurally simple argument supporting and leading to a clearly defined thesis or point of view. Although it will contain certain facts, these should be given to bring out their implications rather than for their own sake. Even if the lecture content is itself inconclusive – unfinished research, for example – the lecturer's presentation should make this quite evident: open-ended subject matter should not result in a lecture that dies out but one that leads deliberately to a conclusion such as, 'More than this we do not know and present research is sustained by the following questions: 1 . . . 2 . . .'. Highly complex arguments should be duplicated and distributed for detailed study, with the lecture as the rallying point for the main issues.

The lecture will generally consist of three or four main parts such as, for example, introduction, collection of data, the lecturer's interpretation of this data, conclusion. The purpose of each part will depend on the lecture but these should be so clearly organised that a member of the audience recalling the lecture would see it in that form.

Whilst the lecture is being prepared care should be taken to check the appropriateness of the vocabulary in which it is written. As a rough guide to their preferred mode of verbal communication, the lecturer could do worse than read the newspapers which his potential audience chooses.

He should also treat facts differently from concepts. If facts are to be remembered they must be presented in such a way as to initiate their learning. They must, of course, be presented unambiguously and this is more likely if the verbal statements are supported by visual aids. The visual and audible sensations should reach the audience simultaneously if this is possible and the fact repeated a number of times after its initial presentation. Any handout should also contain the fact in the same words and any follow-up will aim at over-learning the fact through repetition, encouragement of correct responses and immediate correction of wrong ones.

---

*'The lecture was transferred from the lecturer's notes to the students' notebooks without passing through the mind of either.' *Anon.*

Aids

Line — They won't be effective unless you know what and how they contribute

Perception — reaching out after meaning. act of the intellect: active response to communication
semantic noise

Types: Flat surfaces — chalkboards
feltboards
newsprint
magnet boards
charts and diagrams
overhead projector
film strip
film slide
film loop
film
television — closed & broadcast
models
tape recorder: strip-tape

Projected images —

3-D

ND Vernon's work on interpretation of graphical material

Prof. Ditchburn's work on attention

Box:
1. Line
2. Background
3. Types of aid
4. Particular examples
5. Repeat line

Variations in communications preferences
↳ attitudes, abilities, aptitudes, I.Q. environment

What contribution do they make?
They could ⑥ challenge
② explain words ⎫
③ attract attention ⎬ Concept formation
④ hold attention
⑤ illustrate relationships between +
⑦ ⑥ consolidate, recap, introduce
foster willingness to participate
① attract invite cooperation

Repeat line

Visual Aids

Line (*Improve This*): A teaching aid does not function on its own: it makes a specific contribution to the teaching of something

1. **Background** (a) Everyone is different from everyone else and this affects and includes the preferred mode of communication. Sp. ref. to intelligence and verbal ability: I.Q. curve on felt-board.

   (b) Perception is active response to communication. Involves 'reaching out after meaning.' Examples on O.H.P. (Get response here)

2. **Contributions** What part can aids play in teaching?

   Visual Aids

   (*On felt board*)
   - Invite cooperation – photo of comp.
   - Explain words – tookay slide
   - Attract attention – yellow spot
   - Hold attention – force pump
   - Illustrate relationships – felt graph
   - Challenge – Bernoulli demonstration
   - Consolidate – ref. back

3. **Types of Aids**
   - Chalkboard
   - Felt board ⎫
   - Magnet board ⎬ *Brief use of each in turn*
   - Newsprint pad ⎭
   - Charts
   - O.H.P.
   - filmstrip

Concepts cannot be learned by rote like facts, they are built up in the mind by reorganising facts and other established concepts. It is this process of seeking out understanding that the lecturer must initiate: he must show his group how to go about constructing the concept and indicate to them a way of evaluating their progress towards its full development if this is possible.

Thus, for example, the concept of energy might be introduced with a fact – that energy is the capacity for doing work – followed by references to different forms of energy and examples of energy changes. This might lead to slightly provocative observations such as, 'I wonder if all forms of energy can be traced back to energy from the sun?', or 'Is the world dying a heat death?'

Facts should also be distinguished from opinions and the audience must never be left in any doubt about the validity of an observation which might be one or the other.

Of course, a lecture is an unsatisfactory source of fact-learning and, in general, should not be used for this purpose if an alternative is possible. Nevertheless facts lend an air of veracity to a presentation. Thus the statement, 'This year, three hundred and twenty nine thousand, five hundred and eighteen men and women . . . – about a third of a million people . . .' has the stiff authority of accuracy which is reduced to an easy approximation suitable for retention.

Visual Aids

Visual aids should be considered for the following reasons:

1. By breaking into the verbal flow of the lecture they can revive interest in the occasion itself;
2. They can focus attention on major issues and provide recapitulation or revision in a concise and stimulating form;
3. By presenting numerical data in graphical form they can emphasise its significance or bring out its meaning; and
4. They can give a measure of concreteness to abstract concepts.

The aids which are most appropriate in lectures of this kind are the overhead projector and closed circuit television. They both integrate tightly into the situation and leave control to the lecturer. Films and slides are useful but they introduce a break into the continuity and temporarily relegate the lecturer to a secondary role.

Guidelines to Preparation

Introduction
1. Outline the scope of the lecture and imply (or state) the thesis.
2. Stimulate interest and centre it on the subject.
3. Show the relevance of the subject to the interests of the audience.
4. In general, make the introduction brief.

Body of the Lecture
1. Reduce this to a very few statements (two or three if possible) and prepare to lecture towards each in turn. Accentuate these main statements.
2. Support these main statements from (a) experience, research and so on and with (b) demonstrations or aids and examples.
3. Relax the pressure of information after each main statement.
4. If appropriate (a) present the proposition first, (b) follow through with objections to the proposition and expose their weaknesses and (c) give evidence for the proposition.

Conclusion
1. Retrace the argument very concisely.
2. State the thesis. Try to end in a noteworthy way.

The content should fit into a pressure-of-effort pattern as shown in *Fig.* 5.

Fig. 6 shows the first section of the finished notes for the lecture on visual aids. These will probably not be used in the lecture itself but they will give the lecturer confidence. Certain critical sentences are to be learned by rote and the sequence is signposted by key words on the plan.

Presentation

The test, the only valid test, of a lecturer's competence is his performance and its consequences. In this respect he is comparable with a surgeon who also depends upon extensive preparation and good teamwork. It is amoral to claim to be a lecturer on any grounds other than ability to lecture.

From the moment a lecturer begins, he must try to be as conscious of the effects of his behaviour as a surgeon is conscious of the effects of his knife. During his first few sentences he must work for co-operation. He should rise to his feet and regard his audience as one would rise to greet a friend. He will move naturally but rather more slowly than is his custom in a small room: he will speak more slowly and, if there is no microphone, tune the loudness of his voice to the remote

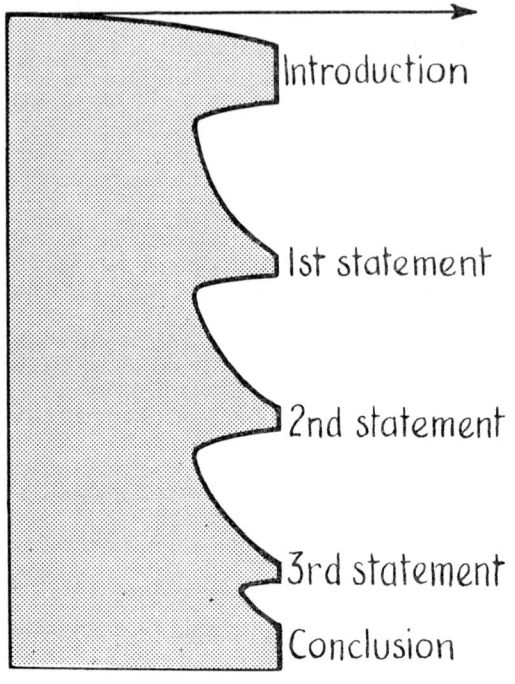

Fig. 5

corners of the hall. He will look at people as he speaks, not with furtive glances but with long straight looks that acknowledge the humanness of the person he sees. He will like his audience: he will not ignore any part of it.

Within a few minutes he should feel the back pressure of the group – their attitude towards him and his subject, their ability to understand, and their interest – and from this moment he can be very closely in touch with every individual except perhaps the few for whom the occasion is unsuitable. When this bond is powerful, each member of the audience associates himself with the lecturer and encourages appropriate responses in the rest of the audience. He enjoys the group approval of the lecturer since he feels that he is partly responsible for the lecturer's competence.

If, on the other hand, the lecture is inadequate, each member rejects the lecturer and associates himself with the audience – the final breakdown is reached when individuals become conscious of the existence of sub-groups to which they can belong when, with signals such as winks, smiles or even spoken observations, they demonstrate their allegiance to other like-minded people who have also rejected any social link with the lecturer.

Since there is no overt feedback, the lecture should be presented in such a way as to evoke active intellectual responses. This involves exploiting verbal techniques; for example, an occasional question followed, after a suitable pause, by the answer; the mid-sentence pause; sentences which end with critical words. These coax or goad or challenge the listeners to anticipate the solution. Here are two examples:

The moment of a force about a point is the product . . . (*pause*) . . . of the force and its perpendicular distance from the point.

A learner's retention is improved by making the consequence of his learning . . . (*slight pause*) . . . satisfying.

The same technique can be used when visual illustrations are employed. To say, 'I will now show you a picture of the broken muscle fibres' evokes visual confirmation whereas if the picture is shown just before the statement, 'This is a picture showing broken muscle fibres' the initial response is one of interpretation which is more active than confirmation. The verbal statement constitutes reinforcement of those interpretations which were correct.

The lecturer should be natural. To prevent movements and gestures from appearing staccato he should make them deliberately and generously. If, for example, it is natural for him to count items on his fingers, he should make it obvious that he is not simply fiddling about. For the most part he should stand still and upright with his head erect. He should breathe more deeply and open his mouth more widely than usual.

Assessment of a Lecture

To improve the standard of his presentation, a lecturer should painstakingly learn from the responses of his audience and the criticism of his peers. It is often useful to invite senior colleagues to attend and to discuss the lecture afterwards. A tape recording can be made and played back, but lecturers are warned that these are often unflattering and should be used with understanding.

The most direct and reliable guides are video-taped records which can be made during lectures on 'home-ground'. These should be discussed with colleagues when they are played back in order to derive the greatest value from them.

The other important source of information is the questionnaire completed by all, or a sample of the audience and, so far as they are concerned,

> VISUAL AIDS
>
> THERE IS A widely held belief that visual aids remove the strain from learning; that in some way they premasticate what would otherwise be intellectually indigestible. Here we are often deceived by the apparent immediacy of visual perception and misled by our own communication preferences.
>
> Learning involves
>
> FELT   SOURCE - RECEPTION = PERCEPTION - COMPREHENSION - KNOWLEDGE
>
> and perceptual ability depends upon a variety of factors, not least of which is intelligence. So during this talk I want first of all to glimpse the background against which visual aids are used, secondly to consider the contribution which aids make to teaching and learning and finally to make a brief survey of the aids which are available.
>
> IQ CURVE   The intelligence spectrum
> ON FELT
>   The relationship between intelligence and preferred mode of communication
>
> High: Verbal, abstraction generalization, technical terms mathematical relationships.
> Low: Need for thing or picture: particular cases, concrete.
>
> In the same way ⌈ the aids we use and how we use them depends on intelligence.
>   ⌊ Also depend on age, ability, experience, environment etc.
>
> OHP   PERCEPTION
>   Now let us see the kind of effect which occurs when we are exposed to visual information.

Fig. 6. Finished notes for lecture on visual aids.

collected by the organisation rather than by the lecturer himself. The following example has been of value to the author:

Questionnaire

Please read the questions below and answer by deleting the words which are not appropriate:

1. Did you find the lecture helpful? No/Fairly/Yes
2. Could you have learned the subject in some other way in the same time? Better/As well/Less ably
3. The lecture period was: Too long/About right/Too short

Please give reasons for your choices in the question below:

4. The section of the lecture which I felt to be most valuable was concerned with . . .
5. The section of the lecture which I felt to be least useful was concerned with . . .
6. The section of the lecture I enjoyed most was concerned with . . .
7. The section of the lecture I enjoyed least was concerned with . . .
8. I would rate this lecture as
   A – lucid, inspiring, absorbing
   B – clear and interesting
   C – a useful experience
   D – difficult and dull
   E – a waste of time

Guidelines to Presentation

1. A dull, sceptical or sleepy audience needs stimulating: increase their pulse rates by making them apprehensive, anxious or amused. An audience which laughs and gradually feels a bite beneath the humour finds relaxation very difficult.

2. If they already understand some of the lecture, tell them so and explain that you are recapitulating: if the lecture is one of a series relate it to the rest.

3. Give guidance on notes, handouts or further reading.

4. Decide the extent to which the audience should be entertained, informed, instructed, encouraged, inspired.

5. Have a 'line', make it known and acknowledge the existence of others.

6. Be prepared to complete the sentence, 'If they have derived nothing else from my lecture, every person now understands . . . (or is able to, or wants, or etc).

7. Collect information about your performance.

BACIE Publications

Prices in brackets are for non-members

AIDS TO INSTRUCTION

A Guide to the Writing of Business Letters. 5th ed., 12th impress., 1969. 24 pp. 53,500 printed.

A step by step guide to the writing of clear and concise business letters, avoiding awkward and old-fashioned 'business English'. Also contains sections on words, sentences and punctuation.

SBN 85171 004 2   5s (8s)

A Guide to the Use of the Telephone in Business. 7th ed., 1969. 21 pp. 35,000 printed.

A helpful guide to all who have to use the telephone, enabling them to check and improve their quality of communication. Prepared with the co-operation of the Post Office.

SBN 85171 001 8   5s (8s)

Report Writing. 2nd ed., 11th impress., 1969. 24 pp. 60,000 printed.

Designed to help those who have to produce business, scientific, or technical reports, 'Report Writing' is chiefly devoted to methods of marshalling facts and ideas coherently, and provides a framework around which to build a clear, logical and orderly report.

SBN 85171 006 9   5s (8s)

Hours into Minutes by *P. J. C. Perry*. 2nd impress., 1967. 30 pp. 10,000 printed.

A guide to committee documentation. Contains specimen documents with a check list to help the Secretary prepare Agendas, Minutes and Supplementary Papers. Illustrated by David Langdon.

           6s (9s)

Tips on Talking. 2nd ed., 9th impress., 1970. 14 pp. 42,500 printed.

Suggestions on the preparation, presentation and shape of a 'talk'. A concise and thoroughly practical guide.

SBN 85171 002 6   5s (8s)

Lecturing to Large Groups by *L. S. Powell*. 3rd impress., 1970. 12 pp. 9,000 printed.

The author vindicates the lecture as an important teaching method and gives detailed guidance on how it can be made purposeful and effective.

SBN 85171 017 4   5s (8s)

A Guide to the Use of Visual Aids by *L. S. Powell*. 3rd ed., 1970. 32 pp. 25,000 printed.

Up-to-date information on the various types of visual aids now available, and the making of aids such as overhead projector illustrations, filmstrips and 8mm loop films. Also includes a list of suggested equipment and publications.

SBN 85171 016 6   7s (10s)

A Guide to the Overhead Projector by *L. S. Powell* 2nd ed., 1970. 48 pp. 16,000 printed.

A concise description of the instrument itself and its use as a training aid, with a detailed explanation of the construction of effective transparencies, diagrams and models.

SBN 85171 010 7   7s (10s)

A Guide to the 8mm Loop Film by *G. H. Powell and L. S. Powell*. 1967. 43 pp. 5,000 printed.

A comprehensive study of 8mm loop films, sources and equipment, with chapters on film-making techniques and the loop film as a teaching aid. Designed specifically for practising teachers and training officers, the book assumes no prior knowledge of film techniques.

           7s (10s)

Multi-Purpose ETV on a Budget by the *Television Research and Training Unit University of London Goldsmiths' College*. 1968. 23 pp. 5,000 printed.

This describes the 'mini-studio', a valuable TV teaching aid which has been evolved with careful regard to economy of cost and space. It gives a step by step guide from the installation of the basic equipment to more advanced systems.

           10s (15s)

Mathematics by Visual Aids. 1962. 48 pp.

A concise booklet describing three-dimensional models used to teach the understanding of simple arithmetical, algebraical and geometrical relationships. The importance of these models lies not only in their effectiveness as teaching aids, but also in the relative ease and cheapness with which they can be constructed.

           5s (8s)

Welcome Stranger by *R. Smurthwaite*. 1968. 18 pp. 25,000 printed, 5th impress.

This booklet gives school leavers a general idea of what to expect—and what will be expected of them—when they start an office job.

SBN 85171 000 X   5s (8s)

Interviewing in Twenty-Six Steps by *J. S. Gough*. 7th impress., 1969. 18 pp. 35,000 printed.

Provides a useful guide on how to conduct a successful interview aided by a check list.

SBN 85171 012 3   5s (8s)

Books for Training Officers. 2nd ed., 1969. 71 pp. 8,000 printed.

An annotated list of 287 publications on commercial and industrial training and other related topics such as industrial psychology, selection and assessment of employees and the transition from school to work. A joint BACIE/National Book League publication.

SBN 85171 008 5   7s (10s)

A Guide to Job Analysis by *T. H. Boydell*. 1970. 32 pp. 2,000 printed.

This book is intended as a practical guide and the theoretical content has been kept to a minimum. Job analysis is placed in its correct perspective in relation to systematic training.

SBN 85171 013 1   15s (22s)